Mary Jackson

Published in the United States of America by Cherry Lake Publishing
Ann Arbor, Michigan
www.cherrylakepublishing.com

Content Adviser: Ryan Emery Hughes, Doctoral Student, School of Education, University of Michigan
Reading Adviser: Marla Conn MS, Ed., Literacy specialist, Read-Ability, Inc.
Book Design: Jennifer Wahi
Illustrator: Jeff Bane

Photo Credits: © Andriy Blokhin/Shutterstock, 5; © NASA, 7; © NASA Langley Research Center, 9, 22; © Everett Historical/Shutterstock, 11; © NASA Langley Research Center, 13; © Joseph Sohm/Shutterstock, 15; © NASA, 17, 23; © Sheila Fitzgerald/Shutterstock, 19; © NASA, 21; Cover, 12, 16, 18, Jeff Bane; Various frames throughout, © Shutterstock Images

Library of Congress Cataloging-in-Publication Data

Names: Loh-Hagan, Virginia, author. | Bane, Jeff, 1957- illustrator.
Title: Mary Jackson / by Virginia Loh-Hagan ; [illustrator, Jeff Bane].
Other titles: My itty-bitty bio.
Description: Ann Arbor, MI : Cherry Lake Publishing, [2018] | Series: My itty-bitty bio | Audience: K to grade 3.
Identifiers: LCCN 2017030505| ISBN 9781534107120 (hardcover) | ISBN 9781534108110 (pbk.) | ISBN 9781534109100 (pdf) | ISBN 9781534120099 (hosted ebook)
Subjects: LCSH: Jackson, Mary, 1921-2005--Juvenile literature. | United States. National Aeronautics and Space Administration--Biography--Juvenile literature. | African American women mathematicians--Biography--Juvenile literature. | African American women aerospace engineers--Biography--Juvenile literature. | Women mathematicians--Biography--Juvenile literature. | Women aerospace engineers--Biography--Juvenile literature. | African American women--Juvenile literature.
Classification: LCC QA29.J33 L64 2018 | DDC 510.92 [B] --dc23
LC record available at https://lccn.loc.gov/201703050

Printed in the United States of America
Corporate Graphics

table of contents

About the author: Dr. Virginia Loh-Hagan is an author, university professor, former classroom teacher, and curriculum designer. Like Mary, she was also born and raised in Virginia and went to the University of Virginia. She lives in San Diego with her very tall husband and very naughty dogs. To learn more about her, visit: www.virginialoh.com

About the illustrator: Jeff Bane and his two business partners own a studio along the American River in Folsom, California, home of the 1849 Gold Rush. When Jeff's not sketching or illustrating for clients, he's either swimming or kayaking in the river to relax.

I was born in Virginia. It was 1921.

I went to school. I learned math.

I learned **science**.

What do you want to learn?

NASA hired me. I started as a "human **computer**." I did math.

My math sent people to space.

Blacks were treated unfairly.
I didn't like it.

I got a new job at NASA.

What do you think is unfair?

I studied **wind tunnels**.
I studied air around planes.

I did tests. I wrote reports.

I wanted to be an **engineer**.
I had to go to a white school.

They let me take classes.

I took classes. I worked hard.

I became the first black female engineer.

I was a Girl Scout leader. I did this for over 30 years.

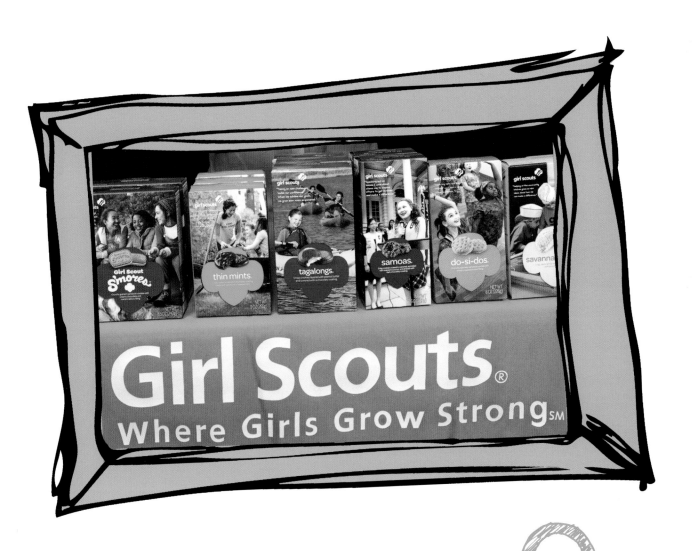

How do you help others?

I died in 2005. I helped blacks. I helped women.

I led the way. I dreamed big.

What would you like to ask me?

1951

1920

Born
1921

1958

2020

↑
Died
2005

glossary & index

glossary

computer (kuhm-PYOO-tur) a machine that can do really hard math problems; a person who can do this is called a "human computer"

engineer (en-juh-NEER) someone who is trained to design and build machines, engines, bridges, or roads

NASA (NASS-uh) the National Aeronautics and Space Administration; it is in charge of the United States' space program

science (SYE-uhns) the study of nature and the world we live in

wind tunnels (WIND TUHN-uhlz) large tubes with air moving inside, meant to copy the actions of an object in flight

index

24